FOREWORD BY
HIS GRACE, THE DUKE OF ATHOLL

It gives me great pleasure to welcome you to HIGHLAND PERTHSHIRE. For anyone visiting, or intending to visit, I am certain this book will prove to be both valuable and interesting.

The breadth of activities available in the area is immense, from the traditional field sports, such as fishing and shooting through bird watching to the more modern pastimes of cycling and hill walking. Many organisations contribute to our local economy: Forest Enterprise, Royal Society for the Protection of Birds, The National Trust for Scotland and Hydro Electric to name but a few. Not only do they employ local people, but the land under their ownership supports a rich diversity of wild bird and animal life. We are fortunate also in having a splendid variety of castles and other buildings, of fine architectural detail, and steeped in history and tradition.

It is with a great sense of pride that I draw your attention to the marvellous photography featured in this book, taken I may add by a local photographer Ronald Weir. Many of the pictures, which portray locations in and around Pitlochry, Blair Atholl and Dunkeld are of aspects of my Estates. I am indeed privileged to be, along with the bodies mentioned above, one of the guardians of such a rich natural and cultural heritage, and I trust you will not only enjoy it, but assist us in preserving it for the enjoyment of others.

We have welcomed many members of Royalty to Highland Perthshire over the centuries, and no matter how short your stay, you are assured as warm and generous a welcome, throughout the district.

Atholl,

INTRODUCTION

HIGHLAND PERTHSHIRE A geological fault line runs through Scotland from Montrose on the north east coast to the Clyde estuary in the west, separating the Lowlands from the Highlands. The Telford Bridge spanning the River Tay at Dunkeld, is known as the Gateway to the Highlands.

Pitlochry lies some 12 miles north of here, a suitable starting point for your exploration of Highland Perthshire.

This guide to Highland Perthshire has been compiled to give the visitor a glimpse of the many attractions that the area has to offer. It does not pretend to be a comprehensive guide, but simply give pointers to various locations which prospective visitors can aim for, and suggests sources of further information.

Local Tourist Offices will gladly provide up–to–date brochures and information, as will hotels and guest houses.

The photographs have been carefully selected not only to show the scenic splendour of the land, but to act as a visual guide, portraying locations that the majority of visitors will be able to reach. For many, a visit to Highland Perthshire will take place during the summer months, when the countryside is lush and green. In selecting the illustrations for this guide it was felt that portraying aspects of all the seasons would allow better insight to the changing moods of this Highland Heart of Scotland.

The publishers acknowledge with grateful thanks the invaluable co–operation of: **His Grace, The Duke of Atholl;** B. Nodes, Administrator Blair Castle; C. Taylor, Tay District, Forest Enterprise; D. Mitchell, Royal Society for the Protection of Birds; J. Todd, Perthshire Tourist Board; N. Bevens, Hydro Electric; Dr A. Barclay, Scottish Wildlife Trust; W. G. Falconer, Burnside Apartments; N. Mitchell, Mitchells of Pitlochry, and all our Advertisers, without whose contribution this book would not have been possible.

CONTENTS

Editorial Contributions: Birds of Highland Perthshire, by D. Mitchell, R.S.P.B.,
Tay Forest Park, by Tay District Forest Enterprise,
Loch & River Fishing, by N. Mitchell, Mitchells of Pitlochry

Designed, Edited and Published by: John MacPherson & Ronald W. Weir.

Map reproduced by kind permission of Bartholomew Maps Ltd., Edinburgh; © Copyright from **Bartholomew Road Atlas of Britain 1994.**

Photography: Ronald W. Weir, 3rd Generation Professional Photographer, specialist in Landscape and Interior Photography. Worldwide agents for stock, travel, calendar and advertising, travelling throughout Europe and America.

Printed in Scotland by Inglis Allen, 40 Townsend Place, Kirkcaldy, Fife KY1 1HF.

TRAVEL TO HIGHLAND PERTHSHIRE

Highland Perthshire, centrally located in Scotland, is easily accessible by road, rail or air.

By road: served by the main A9 route, the area is easily reached from anywhere in the U.K.

By coach: Modern express coach services make it possible to get to Pitlochry from most U.K. cities. Pitlochry is the main terminal for Citylink and National Express in Highland Perthshire. Stagecoach run a local service with other smaller companies running services to outlying areas.

By rail: Linked to the extensive U.K. rail network, connections are easily made to the Highlands and the North through Highland Perthshire. Pitlochry and Blair Atholl have main line stations, many hotels will collect guests by prior appointment.

By air: Glasgow Airport is only 90 minutes away. All the main U.K. and European airlines, and several North American carriers can be connected with. Car hire, coach or rail connections available for your onward journey.

Alternatively Edinburgh Airport, with flights from the U.K. and Europe is only one hour's drive away.

Dundee Airport is only 45 minutes away but has a more restricted service than Glasgow and Edinburgh.

More information can be obtained from your local travel agent, British Rail, or by contacting the Perthshire Tourist Board. Please see Guide to Advertisers (page 56) in this book for useful telephone numbers.

Das Hochland von Perthshire, im herz Schottlands, erricht man genauso leicht per Auto, per Flugzeug sowie der bahn.

Mit dem Auto: über die Schnellstraße A9 kommt man von überall in Großbritannien in die gegend an.

Mit dem bus: moderne Fernbusse verbinden Pitlochry mit den meisten Großstädten. Pitlochry gilt als Endstation für die Buslinien Citylink und National Express. Stagecoach unterhält Ortsbusse und andere Buslinien verkehren in die umiegenden ortschaften.

Mit der Bahn: das Eisenbahnnetz verbindet das Perthshire-Hochland mit dem Norden und dem Süden. Aussteigen darf man entweder in Pitlochry oder in Blair Atholl, wo Hotelgäste nach Absprache abgeholt werden können.

Mit dem Flugzeug: Der Glasgow Flughafan mit Inlandflügen und International flügen nach Europa und Nordamerika liegt nur 90 Minuten entfernt und hat Bus – und Bahnverbindungen sowie Autvermietung für die Weiterfahrt. Nur eine Stunde fahrzeit entfernt liegt der Edinburgher Flughafen mit Inland – und Internationalflügen.

Der Flughafen von Dundee liegt auch nur 45 Minuten entfernt. Der hat aber nur beschränkte Flugverbindungen.

Weit Information erhalten Sie im Reisbüro, beim British Rail oder rufenSie beim Perthshire Tourist Board an. Wichige rufnummer stehen unter Guide to Advertisers (page 56) in diesem Buch.

L'altopiano di Perthshire, al cuore, della Scozia é Facilmentre raggiungibile per autostrada, per ferroia sia per aereo.

Per autostrade: per l'A9 si arriva nella zona facilmente da qualsiasi parte della Gran Bretagna.

Per pullman: gli autobus espressi collegano Pitlochry con tutte le grandi cittá della GB. Pitlochry é capolinea di molti serviza di citylink e National Express. Stagecoach offre servizi locali anche i villaggi remoti sona collegati con servizi di autobus.

Con il treno: Il nord, il sud e l'altopianio di Perthshire sono collegati alla rete ferroviaria. Scesi alla stazione di Pitlochry o a quella di Blair Atholl, chi ha prenotato puô essere accolto dall' al bergaratore.

Per aereo: l'aeroporto di Glasgow si trova a 90 minuti dall'altopiano di Perthshire. Voli da tutte le cittá di Gran Bretagna e voli internazionali atterano qui. Coincidenze ferroviarie e di pullman et autonoleggio.

Meno distante si trova l'aeroporto di Edinburgo con voli interni ed interanzionali. Quelle di Dundee a 45 minuti ha dei collegamenti aerei piú ristretti.

Ulteriori informazioni si trovano dall'agenzia di viaggio, da British Rail o telefonate a Perthshire Tourist Board. Numeri di telefono importanti si trovano nel capitolo Guide to Advertisers (page 56) di questo libro.

▲ GLEN TILT AND RIVER TILT

GLEN FINCASTLE AND BEN A'GHLO ▼

BLAIR ATHOLL

The village is set near the River Garry in Glen Garry, 6 miles north of Pitlochry, amidst some of the most beautiful scenery in Highland Perthshire.

In the immediate vicinity are several places of interest worth exploring. Blair Castle is situated near the village, not more than 15 minutes walk from the entrance gates at the main road. There is a working corn mill open to the public. Glen Tilt is worth exploring, and makes a pleasant walk or mountain bike trip. This scenic Glen with steep sides and an abundance of wildlife, is cut by the clear waters of the River Tilt as it flows down to meet the River Garry. Glen Fender leads up towards Beinn A'Ghlo and can be explored on foot or by car, it offers fine views of Glen Garry and Glen Tilt, with the Falls of Fender tumbling below.

▲ HIGHLAND DANCER

THE TILT HOTEL
Blair Atholl,
Perthshire PH18 5SU

Fax. No. 0796 481335
Tel. No. 0796 481333

Set in the beautiful Vale of Atholl, The Tilt Hotel provides 28 bedrooms (all with private facilities) and has maintained a reputation for traditional Highland hospitality for over 100 years. We pride ourselves in continuing these high standards in the comfortable friendly atmosphere, found only in a family run hotel. Our menu compliments your stay, with local fare, e.g. salmon from the River Tilt, venison from the mountains and glens. For that pre–dinner gathering or after–dinner drink, our well stocked Cocktail Bar is at your disposal, with its excellent range of malt whiskies.
After dinner, on certain evenings why not enjoy a traditional Scottish night with local musicians and singers. Should you prefer a more casual atmosphere, the Roundhouse Bar set in the hotel grounds is a great favourite locally, with its olde world charm, oak beams and stone walls. We will be pleased to send you our brochure on request.

BLAIR CASTLE

CHECK OUT BLAIR CASTLE

Blair Castle is renowned for its outstanding natural beauty, and is the perfect setting for seven hundred years of Scottish history.

Take time to wander through 32 rooms brimming with priceless treasures - then explore the beautiful grounds, and enjoy the rare wildlife that exists in its natural habitat.

Check it out for yourself. Come for the whole day or just a part - Blair Castle is real value for money.

We are open every day from 1st April until the end of October, from 10.00am to 6.00pm. Last admission every day 5.00pm.

For further information, leaflets or party booking forms, TELEPHONE 0796 481207.

Blair Castle,
BLAIR ATHOLL,
PITLOCHRY, PERTHSHIRE

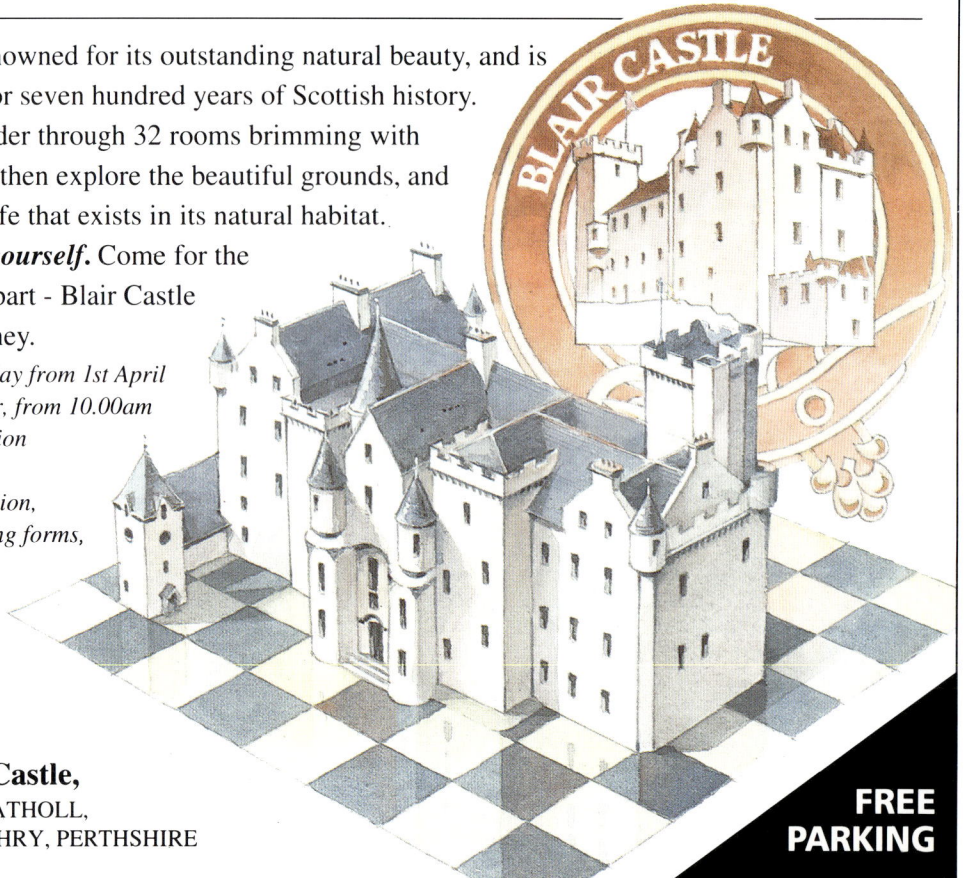

ASSOCIATION
SCOTTISH
VISITOR
ATTRACTIONS
COMMENDED

**FREE
PARKING**

▲ THE DRAWING ROOM
THE RED BEDROOM ▼

▼ THE DININGROOM
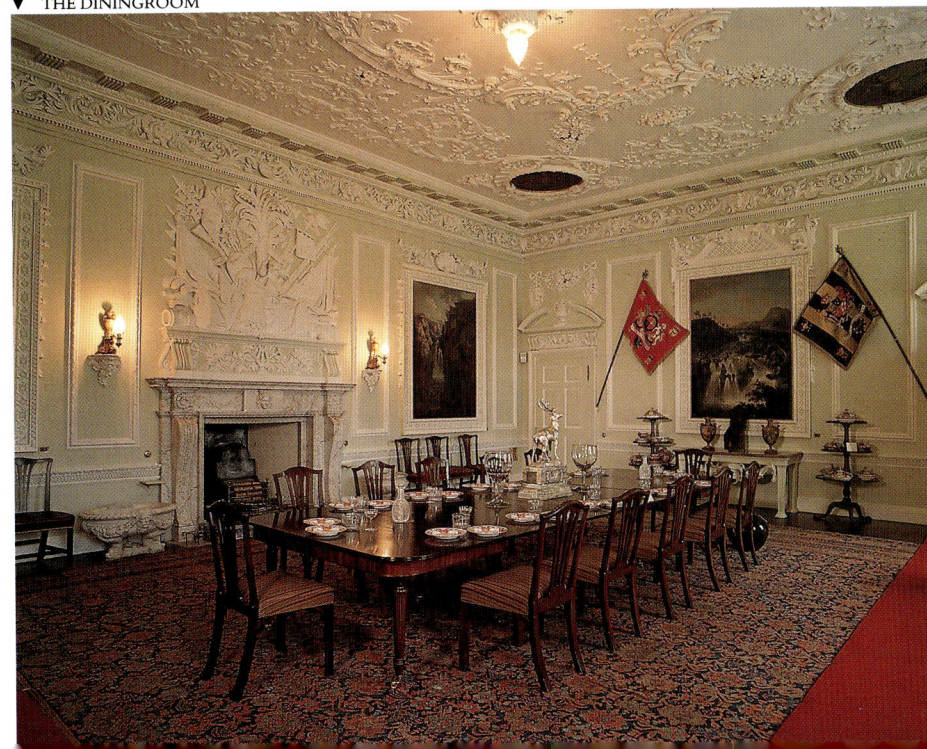

BLAIR CASTLE

Situated in Strath Garry near the village of Blair Atholl, 6 miles north of Pitlochry just off the main A9 trunk road to the north. It lies in a wild setting of fields and woodlands at the foot of the Grampian Mountains. The approach to the castle through the ornate entrance gates from the main road is along the splendid avenue of imposing lime trees. Existing for over 725 years, the castle has withstood siege and occupation on at least four occasions, and has had frequent visits by members of the Royal family. Throughout its history its architectural appearance has changed to reflect individual whims and fancies. Now the home of the 10th Duke of Atholl, the castle is invaded regularly by tourists and is the most-visited privately owned home in Scotland. Rich in history, there are thirty-two rooms fully furnished displaying unique treasures, furniture, a fine variety of paintings, china, arms and armoury and many other fascinating relics covering Scottish life from the 16th Century.

The Drawing Room. Within this magnificent room's wealth of furniture are two gilt settees and twelve chairs made by Chipchase in 1783. Above the fireplace is set the Zoffany Painting of the 3rd Duke and his family.

In 1756 the second Duke furnished this room with a magnificent bed and chairs. The Diningroom presents an image of baroque grandeur, the wall panels are local scenes by landscape artist Charles Stewart, one of the earliest landscape painters commissioned by the 3rd Duke.

Atholl Arms Hotel

Come ye by Atholl

THE ATHOLL ARMS HOTEL is a traditional Highland hotel which has built up its reputation on good food, comfort and friendly service over more than 160 years.

It was built in 1832, the foundation stone of the "New Inn" being laid two years earlier by John the 4th Duke of Atholl, and soon became a principal staging post on the road from London to Inverness.

In 1856 the ballroom was added and this was used for the Duke's private entertainment and for the Atholl gatherings. Being one of Perthshire's premier hotels, it has been patronised by Royalty. In 1844 Queen Victoria visited the hotel and in 1866 Empress Eugene of France, travelling incognito as the Countess de Pierefonds, stayed here.

The hotel is the meeting place for the well known Murray and Donnachaidh Clans.

The recently completed roads from Edinburgh and Glasgow and the direct rail link from London make Blair Atholl easy to reach. The hotel is situated one mile from the main A9 road opposite Blair Castle in the peaceful and picturesque village of Blair Atholl.

Atholl Arms Hotel, Blair Atholl, Perthshire PH18 5SG.
Telephone 0796 481205.   Fax. 0796 481550.

▲ ATHOLL HIGHLANDERS PARADE   BLAIR ATHOLL HIGHLAND GAMES ▼

THE ATHOLL HIGHLANDERS

THE 4TH DUKE OF ATHOLL raised a regiment in 1778, the 77th Atholl Highlanders, to serve with the regular British army for three years during the American War of Independence. Stationed in Ireland until 1783 when they returned home.

QUEEN VICTORIA and Prince Albert stayed at the Castle in 1844 where the Atholl Highlanders mounted a guard for their stay.

1845 saw Queen Victoria present the Atholl Highlanders with their Colours, thus giving them the status of being the only official private army in the British Isles allowed to carry arms.

In past years the HIGHLANDERS have provided Guards of Honour for Royal and Foreign dignitaries. In recent times they have attended Her Majesty at Braemar Highland Gathering, provided a Guard of Honour for His Royal Highness Prince Philip, Prince Charles, and other members of the Royal Family as well as The Crown Prince and Princess of Japan. The present Duke of Atholl started to recruit again and at present their numbers are 50 men and 22 Pipes and Drums.

The Annual Parade of the Atholl Highlanders is held at the Castle in late May and offers a unique opportunity to see the Duke of Atholl's Private Army. The parade is held on a Saturday with the annual Highland Gathering on the Sunday.

TAY FOREST PARK

Set amidst some of Scotland's most spectacular scenery, Tay Forest Park lies at the heart of Highland Perthshire where mountains, rivers, forest and lochs converge to produce an area of outstanding scenic beauty.

Stretching from Loch Rannoch in the west to Dunkeld and the ancient forest of Craigvinean in the east, the Park takes in a diverse network of forests, each with its own character and each offering a sheltered haven for a wide range of wildlife, flora and fauna.

Forest Enterprise, who manage the Park, take great care to balance the commercial and environmental needs of the area with those of the public who are positively encouraged to make good use of the forests and their resources.

A journey through the Park reveals Highland Perthshire at its best with an ever-changing landscape taking in features ranging from the distinctive peaks of Schiehallion and Ben Vrackie to the calm waters of Loch Tay and Loch Tummel. Many visit simply to take in the outstanding views, while outdoor enthusiasts will find plenty of scope for a number of pursuits including cycling, pony trekking and orienteering. Focal point of the Park is the Queen's View Centre which attracts over 200,000 visitors each year. The centre overlooks Loch Tummel adjacent to the famous viewpoint, 'Queens View' named after Queen Victoria who picnicked there in 1866. The recently refurbished centre offers interesting wildlife and forestry exhibitions which set out the full story of the Forest Park and its varied resources. There's also a shop, tea room and popular picnic spot. Walking is probably the most popular pastime with

QUEENS VIEW – LOCH TUMMEL

The Steamie by Tony Roper   Photography by Sean Hudson

PITLOCHRY FESTIVAL THEATRE
Stay six days, see SEVEN plays*

All summer, Pitlochry Festival Theatre offers you a different entertainment almost every night of the week. Choose from classic drama, comedy, farce or a new play. Or stay six days and see them all!

In addition there are art exhibitions, foyer shows, Sunday concerts and craft demonstrations. Drop in for morning coffee with home baking. Our famous buffet lunch – or a "Taste of Scotland" dinner. For a free brochure call 0796 473054.

*from early August

many forests offering a network of waymarked paths with colour coded posts which are graded depending on the gradient and length of the routes. Each walk features different types of terrain and many offer points of interest or spectacular viewpoints. It's also worth taking time to study some of the flora and fauna en route and ornithologists and wildlife enthusiasts will be rewarded with glimpses of common and not-so-common species. Mountain biking is also becoming more popular in the Park where Forest Enterprise is encouraging cyclists to make good use of existing forest tracks. Like the walking routes, mountain bike paths are waymarked and graded with a variety of routes to suit everyone, from a family seeking a breath of fresh air to the more experienced cyclist seeking a scenic challenge. Special waymarked mountain bike routes are now open in Craigvinean Forest near Dunkeld, and at Drummond Hill near Kenmore pony-trekking and field archery also take place within restricted areas; and don't be surprised if a wheeled sled pulled by a team of huskies passes by, some of the forest routes are becoming increasingly popular for husky training and racing.

The forest provides an ideal environment for all types of wildlife, and in some cases positive steps are being taken to conserve and maintain certain species of rare bird or animal.

The Capercaille for instance, distinctive symbol of the Forest park, is currently the subject of long term scientific study which aims to provide information on the birds little understood feeding and breeding patterns.

LOCH TAY AND EVENING MIST

12

The elusive barn owl is also the subject of conservation work as is the goldeneye duck. Attempts are being made to increase the numbers of black and red throated divers by encouraging them to nest on special floating islands installed on lochs within the park.

Pine Martens are becoming an increasingly common site in the park along with wildcats and red squirrel, particularly in the Black Wood of Rannoch, remnant of Scotland's ancient Caledonian Forest, where it is estimated there are over 120 species of moths and butterfly as well as 112 species of spider.

The Tay Forest park has something to offer everyone.

▼ ROE DEER

▲ LOCH TAY AND BEN LAWERS

LOCH TUMMEL IN THE AUTUMN ▼

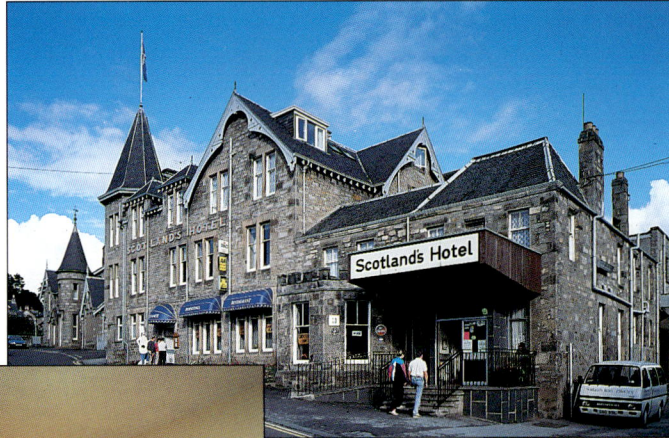

KINLOCH RANNOCH & LOCH RANNOCH

Kinloch Rannoch is a small village sited on the banks of the River Tummel, at the eastern end of Loch Rannoch. The surrounding landscape is dominated by the imposing bulk of Schiehallion; at 3,547 feet this mountain is one of the best known landmarks in the area. Loch Rannoch is a picturesque location at any time of year, but particularly during the autumn when the surrounding woodlands of birch and rowan are a riot of colour. There are many places by the loch to relax and enjoy a peaceful picnic in natural woodland surroundings.

From the south shore of the loch, the many fine stands of native Scots Pines that flourish in the Black Wood of Rannoch can be observed. Rannoch Station is about as far west as one can drive in Highland Perthshire. This lonely outpost, bordering on Argyll district, punctuates the empty vastness of Rannoch Moor which sprawls to Glencoe and the Grampian Mountains. From the Station views of this stark and often dramatic wilderness landscape can be obtained. An important wetland habitat, some 3,500 acres are a designated Nature Reserve. An interesting day trip is to take the train via Corrour, the highest railway station in the British Isles, to Fort William. The magnificent scenery along this route makes it one of the world's finest railway journeys. It is also of interest that during construction of some sections, the rail sleepers were laid on a layer of birch wood to support the line on the soft and unsupportive peat bog of the Moor.

▲ LOCH RANNOCH & SCHIEHALLION

VIADUCT AND STEAM TRAIN – RANNOCH STATION ▼

PITLOCHRY & DISTRICT

Pitlochry, a Highland Victorian town, lies in a beautiful setting in the Tummel Valley surrounded by naturally wooded hills. With its excellent transport links the town is an ideal centre from which to visit Highland Perthshire and many other areas.

East of the town lies Ben Vrackie providing a late summer backdrop of purple heather. Loch Faskally, a man made loch, lies to the west. Dammed for Hydro Power it has a fish ladder with a glass-paneled viewing area through which visitors can see trout and salmon moving up the river.

Just below the dam by the banks of the river is the famous Pitlochry Festival Theatre, within easy walking distance from the town over the dam, or by the suspension bridge across the river. Loch Dunmore, a mile to the north of the town, and set amidst Forestery land, offers excellent walks, sheltered by large conifers and deciduous trees one can follow trails to Loch Faskally, even further to Killiecrankie, or simply stroll around the lochan and return to Pitlochry.

In and around the town are a variety of hotels and visitor attractions. There are many specialist shops offering tweeds, tartans and quality knitwear, and a wide range of local arts and craft goods.

Fine malt whiskies can be sampled in the numerous hotels and pubs, or during a visit to the Blair Atholl distillery, owned by Arthur Bell & Sons.

For the sportsman Pitlochry has much to offer. The golf course welcomes visitors and all professional services are available.

▲ PONY TREKKING

RIVER TUMMEL AND CRAIGOWER HILL, FASKALLY ▼

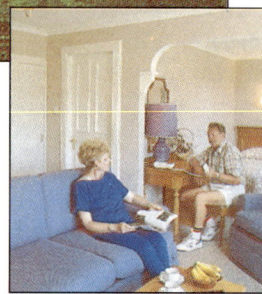

Fishermen are well catered for, with river and loch fishing on offer. Shooting is popular and widely practised. Mountainbiking, walking, climbing, ponytrekking, sailing, canoeing, and during the winter months skiing, can be enjoyed under the expert supervision of skilled guides.

Pitlochry Highland Games are held on the 2nd Saturday of September.

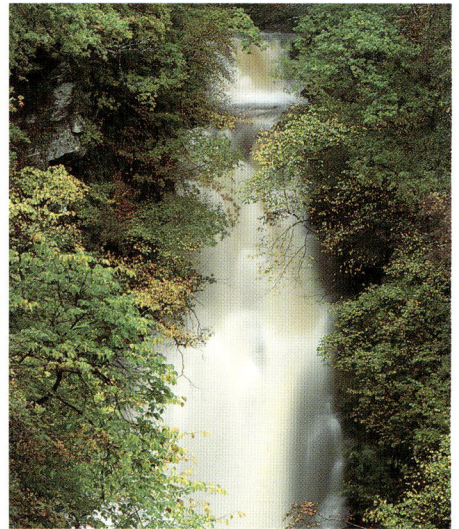

LOCH DUNMORE, PITLOCHRY

BLACK SPOUT WATERFALL

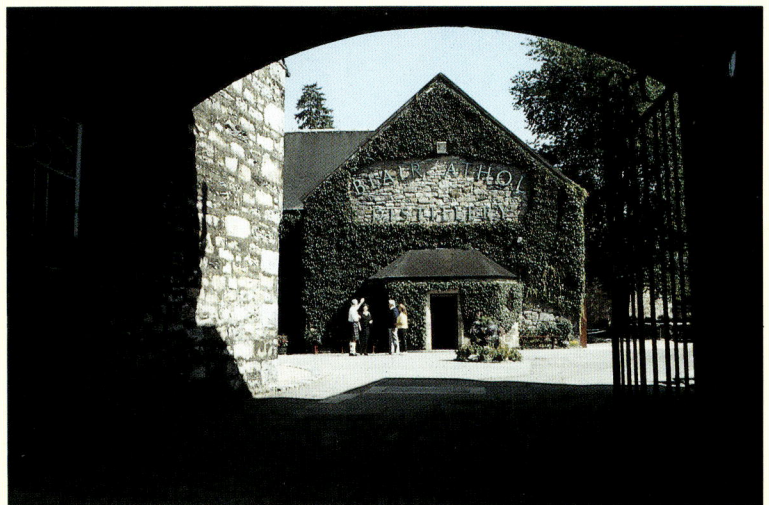

17

LINN OF TUMMEL

The Linn of Tummel, and its woodland, owned by The National Trust for Scotland since 1944, marks the meeting point of the Rivers Tummel and Garry. Derived from the Gaelic 'Linnhe' meaning 'pool', the Linn boasts fine woodland walks, with a splendid variety of flora and fauna.

CRAIGOWER HILL

For the fairly fit, the two hour round trip walk from Pitlochry to CRAIGOWER HILL is a delight. Extensive panoramic views abound. To the north-west towards the famous pass of Killiecrankie, and Blair Atholl. Westwards, and Loch Tummel sparkles in the middle distance whilst far on the horizon the last of winter's snow speckles the hills of Glencoe. Dominating the northern horizon are the peaks of Ben Dearg and Ben a' Chait. Given to the National Trust in 1947 by Mrs D. Ferguson of Baledmund, Craigower Hill, at 1300 feet, was in past times a beacon hill from which fires of warning and celebration were lit. Amongst the abundant flora can be found yellow saxifrage, sundew and butterwort. On the lower slopes of birch, larch and pine many birds and animals such as roe deer thrive.

LINN OF TUMMEL

PASS OF KILLIECRANKIE AND BEN A GHLO

KILLIECRANKIE

The Pass of Killiecrankie, in the 17th century, was the main route north, and it was here in 1689 that an army of men drawn from western Highland clans, and loyal to James VII, were led by John Graham of Claverhouse, Viscount Dundee, into battle against the Government troops under the command of General Hugh MacKay.

MacKay, a veteran soldier, led 3000 foot soldiers and some cavalry into Scotland to quell the Highland uprising against the offering of the Scottish crown to the Protestant, William of Orange and his wife Mary.

Blair Castle, home of the Marquis of Atholl, was seized by Patrick Stewart of Ballechin in the Marquis' absence, and held for the Jacobites. MacKay and Dundee both marched towards Blair; whoever controlled the Castle controlled the Pass, and the route to the north.

On the 27th July, Dundee reached the Castle, and led the Highland army to a commanding position on high ground. MacKay's troops reached the pass within a few hours and when the battle commenced the slaughter began. Within minutes the Government troops under MacKay suffered heavy losses, 2000 men killed or taken prisoner, almost half their army. The Highlanders with only 900 men killed, were victorious, but alas Dundee himself was struck by a bullet in the opening volleys of the fight, and died shortly after.

Today, travellers on the new A9 road can travel through the Pass in minutes. A more rewarding option is to park at the National Trust's Visitors Centre, then take the footpaths which follow the River Garry.

MOULIN

Moulin has the distinction of being the most ancient settlement of the upper Tay, having been in existence for around two thousand years.

A pointer to the importance of Moulin is that it is surrounded by a double ring of fortifications which would indicate a defensive purpose. It is significant that on the hillside above Moulin, across Moulin Moor and extending for some distance east, is one of the largest concentrations of Bronze Age and early Iron Age hut circles in Scotland. Today the village retains a strong sense of history, and boasts many fine buildings such as the Moulin Kirk, the Moulin Inn and cottages. The latter were formerly the coaching hotel, on the old North Road which passed through Moulin until bypassed by the Wade road of 1727.

The Kirk is the oldest in the district, although it has been rebuilt several times, the present building dating from 1875.

Its churchyard contains some gravestones of note, dating as far back as the 12th century. There is also The Black Castle of Moulin, to the east of the village, built around 1325, and inhabited until 1500 when its occupants died from the great plague. A place of considerable atmosphere, the ruins well deserve the name Black Castle.

With its hotel and comfortable bed and breakfasts, Moulin is a good place to relax, enjoy the local fish and game, and perhaps a malt whisky or two.

TUMMEL VALLEY AND BEN VRACKIE

GLEN LYON MOUNTAINS – MIST IN TAY VALLEY

SYCAMORE TREE

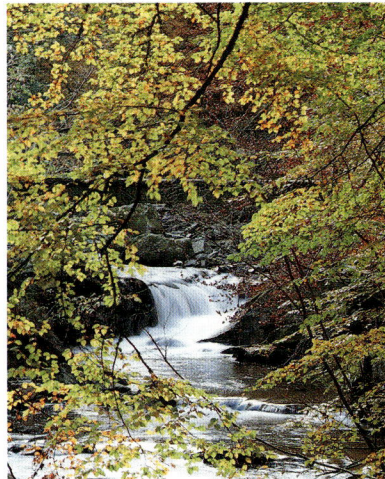
BIRKS OF ABERFELDY

HEARTLAND RADIO IN HIGHLAND PERTHSHIRE FM97.5 MH

Highland Perthshire can boast of having the smallest radio station in Britain, covering an area of 1000 square miles, and serving a population of 12,500, this swelling fivefold during the tourist season.

The transmission serves an area from Dunkeld, Aberfeldy, Loch Tay and Killin over to Loch Rannoch and Calvine, Blair Atholl and Pitlochry, in fact all of Highland Perthshire and beyond, as far as Montrose to the east and Perth to the south.

Tuning into Heartland Radio when on holiday will access programmes which explore local issues and current affairs, information on local events, up-to-date weather and road reports, and music to suit all tastes.

TUMMEL VALLEY AND BEN VRACKIE

▲ TAY VALLEY – MIST AND MORNING LIGHT

▲ SPITTAL OF GLENSHEE

SKIING AT GLENSHEE ▼

KIRKMICHAEL

KIRKMICHAEL village lies east of Pitlochry, through Glen Brerachan where the road climbs steeply past Moulin, attaining a height of 1,260 feet. The village nestles in Strath Ardle by the River Ardle, surrounded by hills and woodlands. Near the village lies Blackcraig Castle with its unusual Bridge Lodge which straddles the bridge over the River. The area surrounding Strath Ardle has a rich and colourful history going back to the Picts, and over the centuries various fortresses and strongholds have been built, each with its own tales and legends.

From Kirkmichael the road joins the main road (A93) in Glenshee before heading north to The Spittal of Glenshee and into Deeside. Glenshee Ski Centre, on the border of Grampian Region is the most extensive ski centre in Scotland offering 28 ski lifts servicing three valleys. The ski season extends from December through to April.

Ski hire and excellent instruction is available at the Centre and from several establishments within the Glen.

POWER FROM THE GLENS

Hydro-Electric's Tummel Valley catchment area extends over 1,839 sq. km. of the Grampian Mountains, and contains some of the most rugged and remote parts of the Scottish Highlands. With an installed capacity of 245 megawatts, and an average annual output of 459 million units of electricity, the system makes a major contribution to the National Grid. Amongst the many generating stations which Hydro-Electric maintain, the power station below the Gaur Dam, fed with water drawn from the desolate Moor of Rannoch by the River Gaur, has the distinction of being the first one in Scotland to be fully automated, with its operation controlled by the water level in Gaur Reservoir. The numerous installations which comprise the Tummel system are now all operated by remote control from the Hydro Group Control Centre at Errochty. Situated on the River Tummel, where it is joined by the River Garry, Clunie power station, the Control Centre is a good example of Hydro-Electric's environmental commitment to maintain as discrete a presence as possible throughout the district. Carefully landscaped and screened by trees, the Centre and associated buildings are well hidden, ensuring the scenic splendour of the location remains intact.

Of all the visitors who stop at Queens View, to enjoy the splendid views over Loch Tummel, very few realise that the loch is a major contributor to the Hydro-Electric's generating capacity.

▲ FASKALLY DAM, PITLOCHRY AND RIVER TUMMEL

▼ SCHIEHALLION, RIVER TUMMEL AND FALLS

Perhaps the most visited loch, and certainly one of the most attractive, is Loch Faskally at Pitlochry. A man-made loch, it is the last one in the system and therefore handles water which may have generated electricity at three or four other power stations before reaching this point. The scenic beauty of Loch Faskally and the dam with its fish ladder are now a major tourist attraction, listed amongst the top five in Scotland. More than half a million tourists cross the dam each year and 150,000 enter the Visitor Centre in the dam. The viewing chambers in the salmon ladder allow visitors to watch salmon running upriver to spawn, using the ladder to bypass the dam. Hydro-Electric therefore enjoys a unique position in Perthshire. Not only does it provide direct benefits to the local economy by employing hundreds of local people, it makes a significant contribution to the tourist industry through its position as careful custodian of many areas of environmental importance.

HYDRO ELECTRIC DAM – LOCH FASKALLY & RIVER TUMMEL ▼

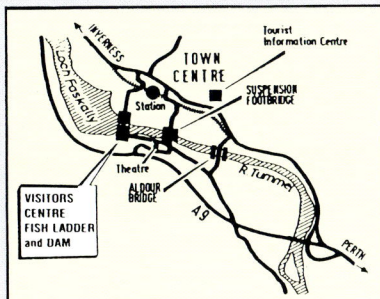

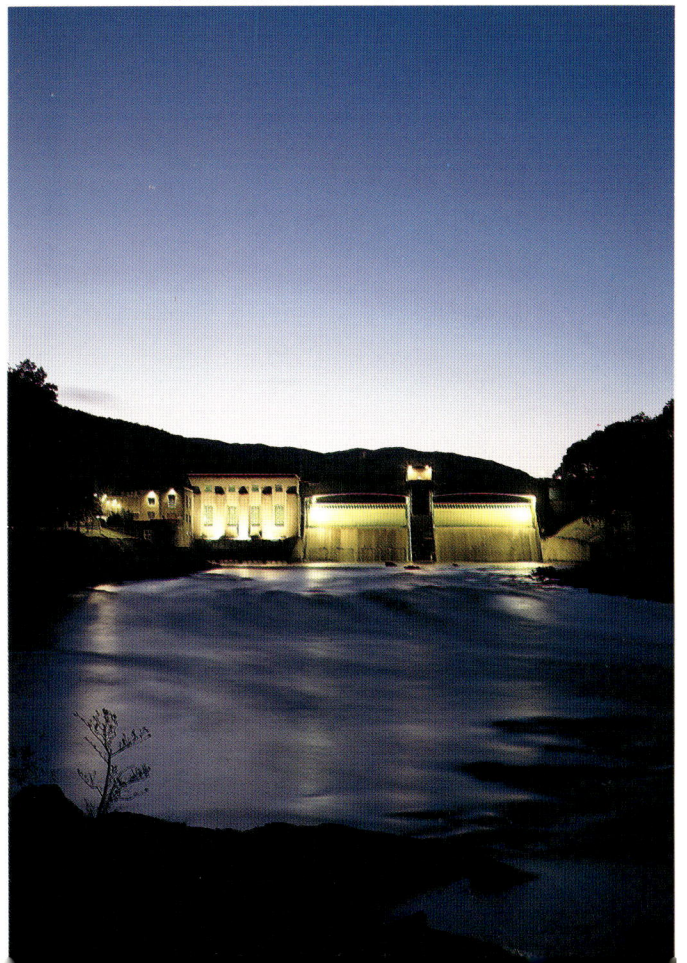

25

DAY TRIPS BY CAR

THE TROSSACHS

From PITLOCHRY head for ABERFELDY, home of a splendid example of Wade Bridge, named after General George Wade who was ordered to construct a system of metalled roads to police the southern Highlands, following the Jacobite Rising of 1715. Here also is the Black Watch Monument which commemorates the origins of the famous regiment. Winding alongside scenic Loch Tay, the road enters THE TROSSACHS and countryside made famous by the exploits of Rob Roy. To the west by Loch Achray the road leads to the woodland fringed hills surrounding Loch Katrine, a jewel amidst lochs. Passing Aberfoyle the road arrives at DOUNE CASTLE, one of Scotland's finest mediaeval castles and home, for 400 years, to the Earls of Moray. Within the Castle's estate is a splendid motor museum with many fascinating exhibits. A short drive through lush and fertile farmland provides an unusual spectacle for Scotland – lions, monkeys and other African mammals in the BLAIR DRUMMOND SAFARI PARK. Returning to a more urban setting we reach STIRLING, overlooked by historic STIRLING CASTLE, and nearby the famous BANNOCKBURN where Robert the Bruce and the small Scottish army soundly defeated the English troops in 1314. Through Dunblane and Crieff the road follows the River Almond as it winds along the Sma' Glen. A short drive through Dunkeld leads back to PITLOCHRY, for a few miles on the old A9, heading north, this road offers fine views of the Tay Valley before meeting the main A9.

Approx. distance 160 miles.

CASTLE MENZIES

From PITLOCHRY the road to Royal Deeside follows one of the highest routes in Britain, reaching 2,200 feet up into the Grampian Mountains. In Winter the area draws skiers from all over Scotland, but even in summer the occasional snow flurry is not unusual. Grouse croak amongst the heather, and red deer can often be spotted on the higher tops. Descending to BRAEMAR the bare moorland is left behind as the road drops into mixed woodlands. Home of the famous Highland Gathering, Braemar nestles amidst classic Highland scenery. To the East is BALMORAL, summer residence of royalty since the Victorian era. Not far away is Crathie where the Royal Family attend the little church whenever they are in residence. The road twists and turns on through Ballater and Aboyne, through Banchory, to CRATHES. Crathes Castle, owned by The National Trust for Scotland, and reputed to be haunted, will amply reward those who take the time to explore its fascinating interior, and walk amongst the extensive gardens. To the South the road passes Bridge of Feugh and Fettercairn, arriving at EDZELL. An unusual sight here is the Renaissance-style walled garden which dates from 1604. Through Brechin the road reaches KIRRIEMUIR, birthplace of J. M. Barrie, creator of Peter Pan. Heading West again the road passes through picturesque Glen Isla to return to PITLOCHRY.

Total Distance approx. 160 miles.

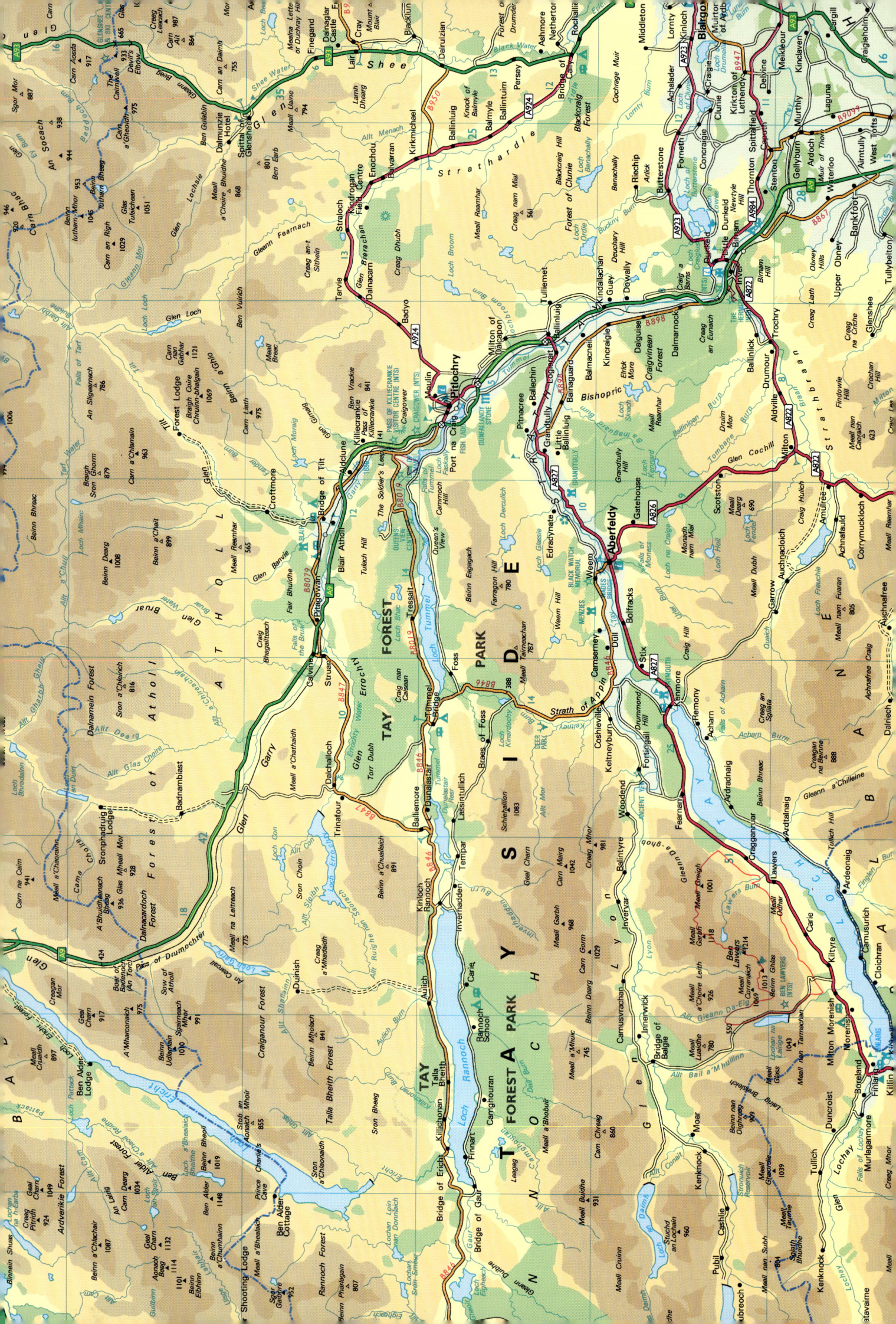

Blairgowrie · Rattray · Meikleour · Kinloch · Kirkton of Lethendy · Murthly · Stanley

Dunkeld · Birnam · Dalguise · Dowally · Ballinluig · Logierait · Pitlochry · Moulin

Aberfeldy · Weem · Dull · Fortingall · Kenmore · Lawyers · Killin

Pitlochry · Killiecrankie · Blair Atholl · Bridge of Tilt · Calvine · Struan

Kinloch Rannoch · Tummel Bridge · Foss · Aulich · Kilvrecht

TAY FOREST PARK

FOREST OF ATHOLL

Loch Tummel · Loch Rannoch · Loch Tay · Loch Errochty · Dunalastair Water

Glen Lyon · Glen Garry · Glen Tilt · Glen Lochay

Ben Lawers · Meall Corranaich · Schiehallion · Ben Vrackie

A9 · A924 · A923 · A984 · A827 · A826 · B8019 · B8079 · B846 · B847

▲ LOCH TAY

LOCH FASKALLY ▼

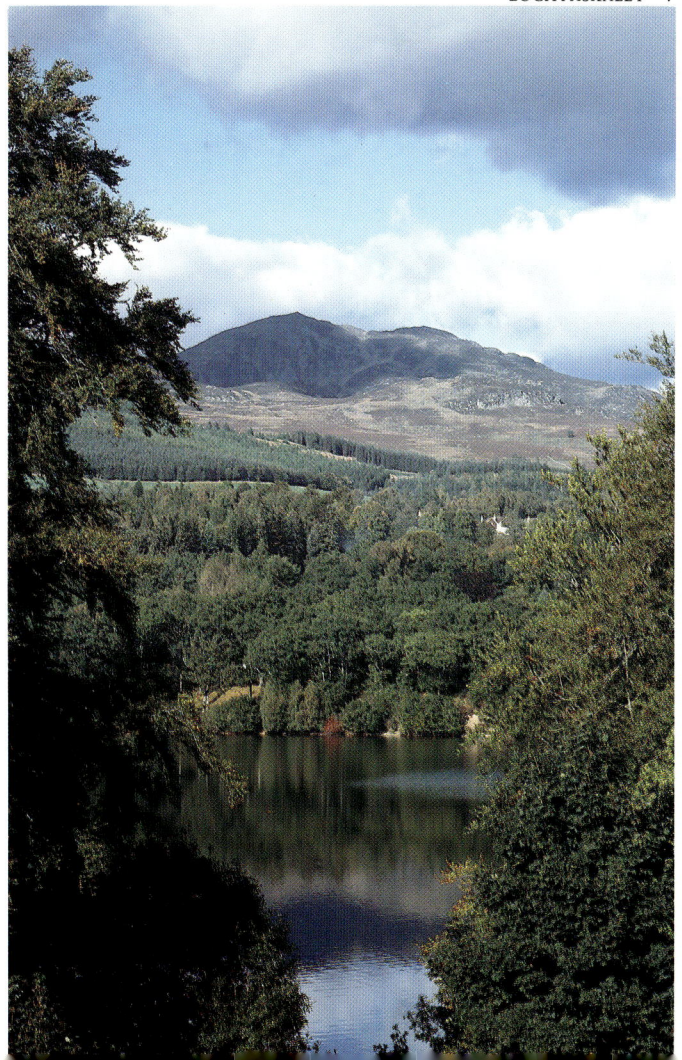

KIRRIEMUIR & GLAMIS

Leaving PITLOCHRY the road heads through MOULIN and quickly climbs to nearly 1300 feets before descending to Glen Brerachan. A short stop in KIRRIEMUIR will allow a visit to the birthplace of J. M. Barrie, creator of Peter Pan, now owned and preserved by the National Trust for Scotland. Heading south the route brings you to GLAMIS, and the magnificent baronial GLAMIS CASTLE. Adorned with towers and turrets the castle contains a splendid collection of paintings, tapestries and furnishings, and was the childhood home of the Queen Mother and the birthplace of Princess Margaret. A visit to the Angus Folk-Museum in Glamis village will provide an interesting and educational insight into the life of previous generations.

Continuing to Meigle, Coupar Angus and Blairgowrie we arrive at DUNKELD, an ancient cathedral town and renowned for the beauty of its setting. Wordsworth, Queen Victoria and Robert Burns have all enthused about Dunkeld. The National Trust for Scotland has undertaken some fine restoration work on CATHEDRAL STREET and welcomes visitors. The return drive to Pitlochry follows first the River Tay and then the Tummel, as they wind their way through the tree lined glen.

Approx. distance 85 miles.

▲ LOCH DUNMORE

PITLOCHRY FESTIVAL THEATRE ▼

30

▲ FARMING EAST HAUGH   FARM HOUSE NEAR WEEM, ABERFELDY ▼

STRATHSPEY

This route climbs through DALWHINNIE with its lonely distillery, to NEWTONMORE.

Not far from the village is the HIGHLAND WILDLIFE PARK, where many examples of Scottish wildlife are on display in authentic surroundings. AVIEMORE centre of the winter sports industry sits amidst vast expanses of native pinewoods, home to deer, wildcats and various birds of prey. BOAT OF GARTEN is world famous for its osprey nesting site, and the RSPB reserve there offers a closed-circuit video view of the ospreys as they rear their young, or alternatively watch with binoculars as these elegant birds arrive with trout from the nearby lochs and streams. GRANTOWN ON SPEY is well known to fishermen of the human variety and anglers come from all over the world to fish the mighty River Spey.

Climbing steeply into the Grampian Mountains to TOMINTOUL the route twists and turns amidst dramatic scenery and this road has the unenviable reputation of being amongst the first closed when winter snows begin to pile up. Descending steeply to Deeside, BALMORAL and BRAEMAR, the road returns through Glen Clunie, to the Devil's Elbow and Glenshee, then west to Kirkmichael and PITLOCHRY.

Approx. distance 145 miles.

GLENCOE

From PITLOCHRY we pass through ABERFELDY and along the shore of Loch Tay, to KILLIN. At CRIANLARICH we head north to Tyndrum, and begin the ascent towards Rannoch Moor and Glencoe. Vast expanses of open moorland stretch away all around to rugged mountains, and a visit to the GLENCOE SKI AREA CHAIRLIFT will allow an easy ascent to give dramatic and extensive views over the sprawling moor. Red deer can be spotted at any time of year and occasionally a golden eagle may be sighted spiralling high on thermals. There is also an interesting museum of climbing located here, with equipment and photographs. GLENCOE itself is infamous, as the site of one of the most barbaric incidents in Highland history. Here in 1692 troops under the command of Captain Robert Campbell of Glenlyon enjoyed the hospitality of the MacDonalds for several days before suddenly turning on their hosts during the darkness of 13 February, and slaughtering without mercy thirty eight people, including women and children.

Following the shores of Loch Leven and Loch Linnhe we reach FORT WILLIAM with its dramatic backdrop of mountains. Dominated by BEN NEVIS, at 4406ft. the highest mountain in Britain, the surrounding peaks offer climbing, walking and wildlife viewing. In winter the town is transformed into a bustling ski resort and in summer the covered gondola system, the only one of its type in the U.K., at the AONACH MOR SKI AREA allows access to the mountain where lunch accompanied by stunning views can be had in the mountain restaurant.

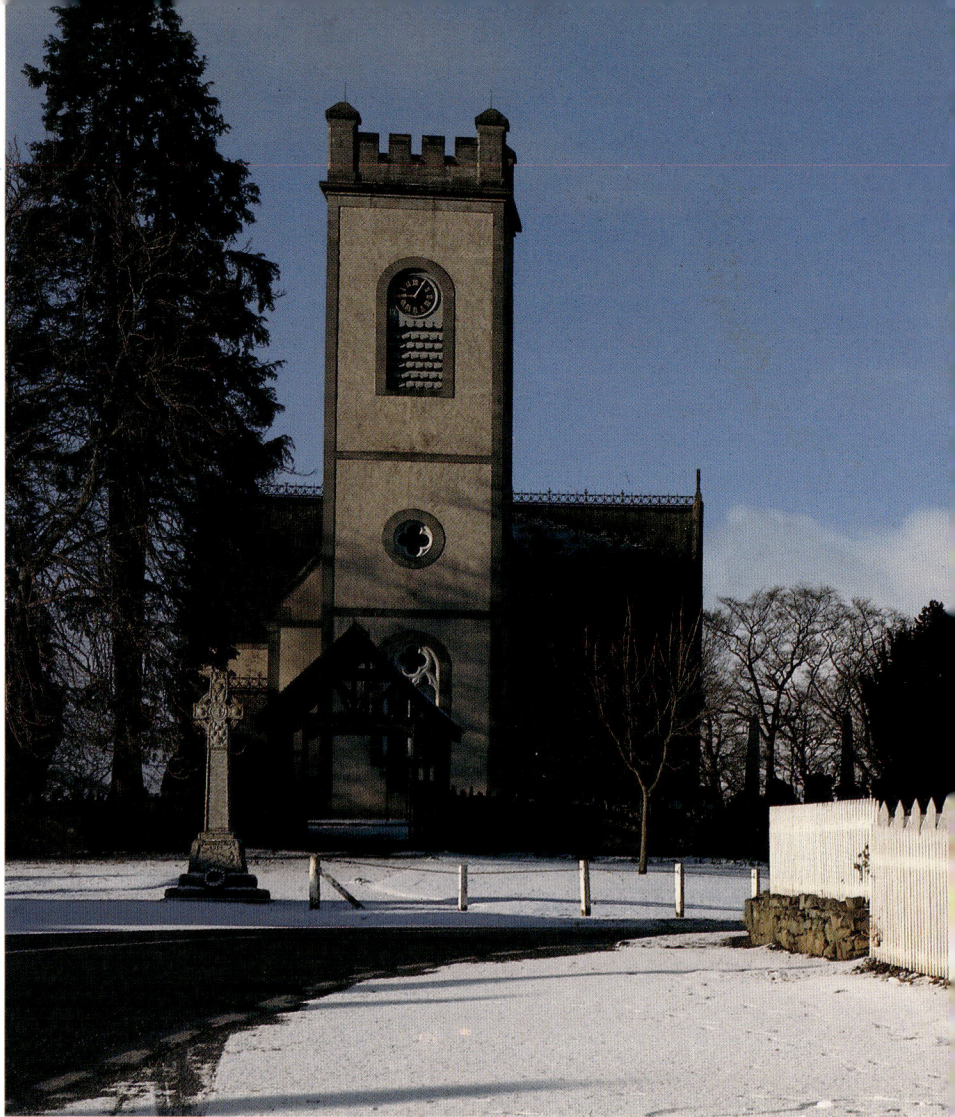

▲ KENMORE VILLAGE

▼ SCHIEHALLION FROM NEAR KENMORE

In Fort William town the WEST HIGHLAND MUSEUM is famous for the "secret" portrait of Bonnie Prince Charlie, painted as a curved smudge and only visible when a silver goblet is placed at its centre. Heading North the road forks at SPEAN BRIDGE and follows Loch Laggan, leaving behind the rugged glaciated peaks of the west and entering the more rolling hills of Perthshire. Through BLAIR ATHOLL and past the imposing BLAIR CASTLE then the PASS OF KILLIECRANKIE, the road returns to PITLOCHRY. Approx. distance 175 miles.

BIRDS OF NORTH PERTHSHIRE

Perthshire, lying across the boundary between lowland and upland Scotland, is home to a great variety of birds.

Examples of Scotland's most important wildlife habitats, apart from the sea coast, are found in Perthshire, and the resultant varied landscape similarly boosts the number of birds of different kinds to be found there.

The fertile straths and the floors of the glens hold a large number of birds, waders, oystercatchers, lapwing and snipe, while common sandpiper, dipper and grey wagtail appreciate the clarity of the area's rivers and burns. Some of Scotland's finest oak woods are found on the glen sides. One superb example, at Killiecrankie, is the R.S.P.B. Nature Reserve. On fine mornings in early May these woods are alive with birdsong. Wood and garden warblers competing, and both striving to outdo the redstart. Together these blend to form a magical natural harmony. Higher up, above woods and grassland, much of the landscape is heather moorland. Some of the finest grouse moors in Britain are in Highland Perthshire. These vast tracks of ling heather are carefully managed to maximise red grouse numbers but many other birds benefit also.

North Perthshire is the heartland in Britain of the Black Grouse and would also hold good bird of prey populations.
However illegal trapping, shooting and poisoning are very common, taking a heavy annual toll of hen harrier, buzzard, peregrine and golden eagle.

MIST AND AUTUMN, LOCH TUMMEL

▲ AUTUMN MIST, BEECHWOOD, DUNKELD.

These birds have supposedly enjoyed legal protection for many years and all sensible people must condemn the wanton persecution they endure.

The osprey is doing well in Highland Perthshire however, and is now a common site on many lochs and rivers in the area. Travellers on the A9 often see these beautiful birds hovering over the River Tay. Osprey are often disturbed in their tree top eyries by careless birdwatchers, so if you come across a nest-site, by all means admire from a distance but then pass by carefully. The R.S.P.B. would like to hear of osprey eyries anywhere in the country so that they can be protected from egg-collectors who in some years have robbed nests in Scotland of a quarter of all eggs laid.

Please refer to Loch of the Lowes for more information on the osprey.

▼ WATERFALL IN AUTUMN NEAR PITLOCHRY.

DUNKELD

Nestling comfortably amongst rolling wooded hills, DUNKELD is a popular holiday destination for many hundreds of visitors who enjoy its historic charms. Situated on the banks of the River Tay the town boasts a fine example of Telford Bridge, dating from 1809. Following destruction during the battle of 1689, the town was rebuilt in the 18th century by the Dukes of Atholl and more recently by the National Trust for Scotland and Perth County Council in 1950 and 1960.

The town has much of historical and architectural interest for the enthusiast to explore, such as its unusually shaped square around the market cross and the restored cottages on Cathedral Street. Embedded in the wall of The Ell Shop is the 'ell', the weaver's measure possibly positioned there for the convenience of customers at market time.

The ancient cathedral lies at the top of Cathedral Street, dating from the 12th and 15th century, in well kept grounds by the river. The choir open to visitors, this historic cathedral is now used as the Parish Church.

In the immediate vicinity of Dunkeld are numerous sites of interest, such as The Hermitage, and there are a variety of woodland walks to explore.

▲ DUNKELD AND CATHEDRAL

▲ CATHEDRAL

THE ATHOLL ARMS HOTEL
BRIDGEHEAD
DUNKELD PH8 0AQ
Telephone 0350 727219

A Georgian coaching Inn built in 1790, over-looking the river Tay and Dunkeld Bridge.

There are 20 bedrooms, dining room to seat 35 guests, a fine function room on the first floor.

An extensive and reasonably priced menu, is served both in the dining room and lounge together with a wide range of beers, wines and spirits.

THE ELL SHOP, DUNKELD ▼

▲ SYCAMORE AND MAPLE TREES, AUTUMN COLOUR

SUNRISE OVER LOCH CLUNIE ▼

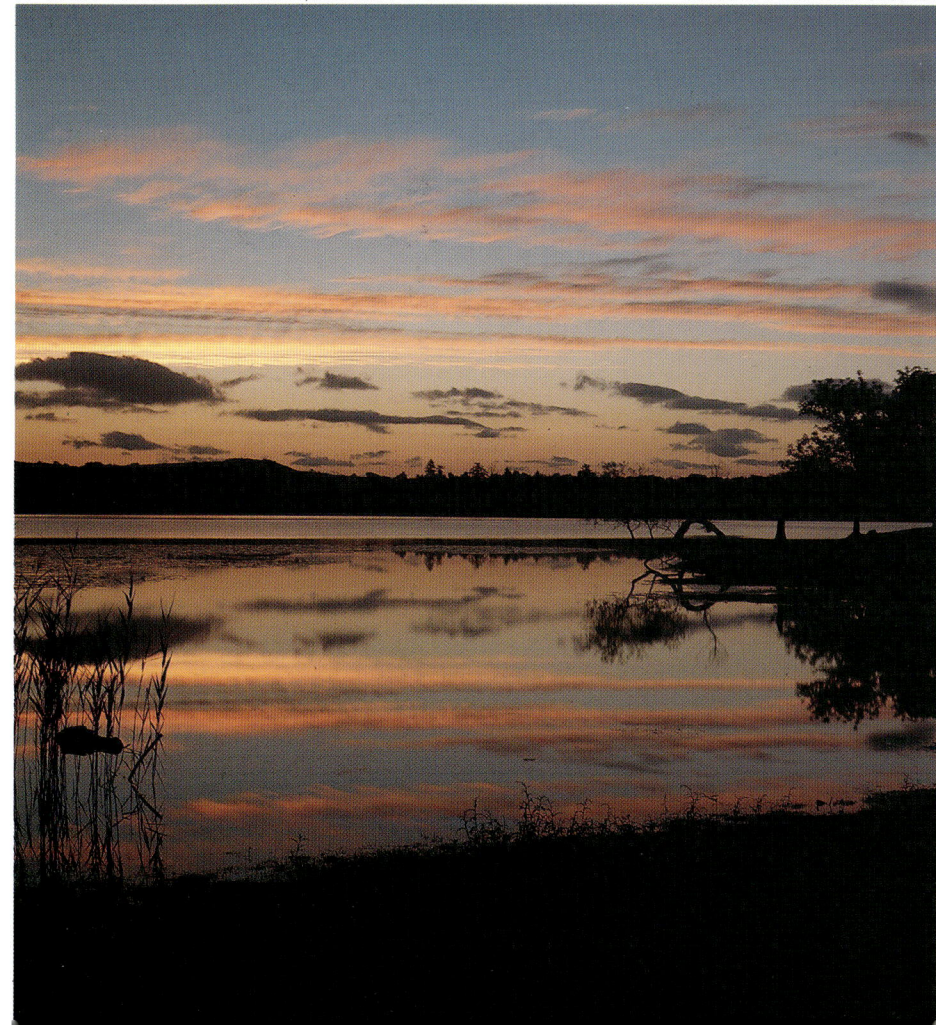

LOCH OF THE LOWES

Situated 2 miles east of Dunkeld, the Loch of the Lowes Wildlife Reserve and Visitor Centre has been designed to enable visitors to watch wildlife without disturbing it, and to learn more about the diversity of flora and fauna of the Reserve from the resident Ranger/Naturalist. With its fine mix of wooded hills and wetlands the Reserve supports a rich variety of plant life. Amongst the animals to be seen are deer, both roe and fallow, squirrels and many others. In recent years otters have been seen occasionally, and are now appearing more frequently. For many visitors the highlight has been a view of the magnificent osprey as it lands on its nest, a large trout writhing in its razor-sharp talons, and destined to fill the bellies of its hungry chicks.

An observation hide, well-equipped with binoculars, is available during opening hours, and has suitable access for disabled visitors.

Attracting in excess of 30,000 visitors every year, the Loch of the Lowes has earned its place as one of the premier natural attractions in Highland Perthshire.

OSPREY

NEAR DUNKELD · RIVER BRAN · THE HERMITAGE

WOODLAND HERMITAGE

RIVER BRAN, NEAR DUNKELD ▼

THE HERMITAGE

A mile west of DUNKELD on the Perth – Inverness road lies The Hermitage Woodland.

This splendid wooded area covers over 35 acres and contains numerous native and exotic trees. Year round it offers sights and sounds to captivate the senses. In Spring bluebells carpet the woodland floor and perfume the air. Summer brings dense and lush greenery and the hum of insects, before the shorter, sharper Autumn days paint a riot of red and gold. The occasional glimpse of roe deer nosing amongst the leaf litter, or red squirrels scurrying for cover, will reward those whose approach is quiet and careful. The Hermitage folly, or Ossian's Hall, was built in 1758 by 2nd Duke's nephew as a surprise for the Duke, and has unfortunately suffered badly since from vandalism, although in recent years much restoration work has been undertaken by The National Trust for Scotland. The waterfall roaring below when rain swollen in wet weather provides an imposing backdrop, and in the Summer, sunshine filtering through the trees forms delicate rainbows in the spray. Amongst the birdlife resident in the woodland are Grey Wagtails, their bright yellow undersides flashing as they pursue insects. One of the most appealing birds is the Dipper. This delicate, white breasted bird sits on its favourite rock, bobbing up and down before diving under the water surface to pursue insect larvae. Wood pigeons clatter noisily through the branches, while the high-pitched call of Goldcrests, Britain's smallest birds, pierces the dense woodland canopy. Adequate and well maintained paths are maintained and there is also access for the disabled.

▲ TAY VALLEY, NORTH OF DUNKELD

DOWALLY FARM

**Self catering
holiday accommodation**

**Proprietor: Mrs Kathleen Laird,
Dowally Farm, Ballinluig, Pitlochry,
Perthshire PH9 0NR.**

Telephone 0350 727475

Situated in the Heart of Perthshire overlooking the River Tay, these cottages are fitted out to a high standard. Colour TV, electric heating, microwave and washing machine.
All bed linen is provided.
Ideal situation for touring, golf, fishing and lovely walks.
We will be happy to send you our brochure by return on request.

▲ TAY VALLEY NEAR DOWALLY

DOWALLY

This small village lies just off the A9 road, 5 miles north of Dunkeld. For the visitor wishing to relax and enjoy the pleasures of fishing and walking, Dowally is an ideal base. There is a tremendous variety of wildlife in the surrounding hills which are part of Atholl Estates, and even the rare and elusive osprey can occasionally be spotted fishing on the numerous lochs. Car parking is best found on the old A9 within the village, near the craft shop.

▲ RIVER TAY

DOWALLY CHURCH ▼

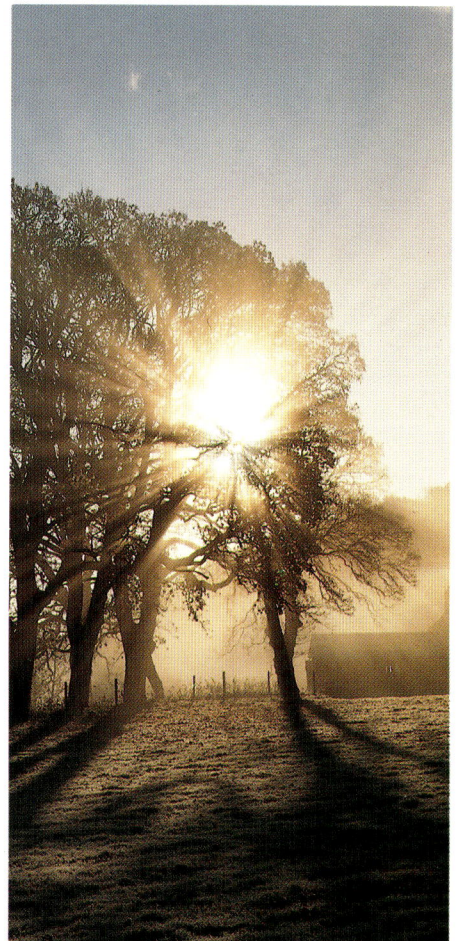

St Anne's Kirk
DOWALLY
Sunday Service 2 pm
Next Week

OLD ROMAN BRIDGE – GLEN LYON

▲ TAY VALLEY AT LOGIERAIT

CELTIC CROSS – SUNSET ▼

LOGIERAIT

Logierait stands at the junction of the Rivers Tay and Tummel, and takes its name from the Gaelic, Lag-an-Rait, meaning Hollow of the Fortress. The site of the fort is marked by a Celtic cross visible on the right as you cross the River Tummel. There are many sites of historical interest in and around the village, amongst them Logierait Church. The present building dates from 1805, but the location has had significance since 650AD when St. Cedd established a religious site here, blessing a nearby spring. Logierait was once known as Lag-an-mo Ched, meaning Hollow of beloved Ched.

ABERFELDY

Aberfeldy has numerous sites of interest for the visitor. Despite its modest size the town and its surroundings will provide many hours of pleasure for those who take the time to explore. One of the finest features of the town is the Wade Bridge, elegantly spanning the River Tay.

Not far away is the Black Watch Memorial which commemorates the raising of this famous regiment. The golf course is situated next to the river and Wades bridge. Aberfeldy Water Mill, beautifully restored, and working, has an audio-visual display, and there is also Aberfeldy Distillery, in production since the 1840's. There are some fine shops in Aberfeldy, specialising in local arts and craft products, and for the more energetic the Aberfeldy Recreation Centre offers a variety of sports and an indoors swimming pool. Just outside the town, close to the village of Weem, is Castle Menzies. Built in the 16th century, this is an excellent example of a z-plan fortified tower, and is undergoing long-term restoration work.

There is car parking, reception, toilets and a shop provided. Weem itself is one of the oldest settlements in the area, records indicating its status as the centre of a parish from 1235.

There are numerous events of interest to the visitor, in and around Aberfeldy each year.

WADE'S BRIDGE, RIVER TAY

The Aberfeldy Gala Week is held in June, as is the Provincial Gaelic Mod (festival/competition of Gaelic music, song and dancing); and in various locations there are Highland Games during July and August.

GRANDTULLY

Mention Grandtully to any whitewater canoeist and they smile! The River Tay, flowing over a spectacular series of rapids here, has created one of the finest natural slalom sites in the country. The Scottish Canoe Association, who govern the sport in Scotland, organise several large events each year, attracting over two hundred competitors. However, for the recreational canoeist there is ample fun to be had, with paddling to suit all abilities. For those who prefer their fun with the entire family, a recent introduction from the USA is the sport of white water rafting using large rubber inflatables in which to bounce down the river in relative comfort. As well as being exciting it also allows an opportunity to see the surrounding countryside from a unique viewpoint. Grandtully village itself developed around a mill, downstream from the Strathtay Bridge, with water from the river powering the wheel. With the construction of the bridge spanning the Tay in 1869, the opposite bank of the river was opened for development and soon numerous villas were built, used mainly as holiday homes for the wealthy.

Thus developed the village of Strathtay.

KENMORE AND LOCH TAY

Kenmore village, at the head of Loch Tay, grew up around an inn which was built on a croft in 1572 by Colin Campbell, one of the Campbells of Glenorchy, who owned substantial estates in the district and as far west as Oban. This inn now forms the main part of the present Kenmore Hotel. Within 100 years a settlement had formed around the inn, with a church and numerous cottages. Towards the east end of the village is a splendid archway which marks the entrance to Taymouth Castle. The castle is set amidst extensive grounds, designed and created during the reign of the second Earl (1662 - 1752). Taymouth Castle Golf Course is within the Castle grounds. Loch Tay itself is a popular location for visitors, particularly lovers of water sports, with sailing, windsurfing, waterskiing and canoeing all available. The loch has supported communities for centuries, and the earliest inhabitants lived on man-made islands known as crannogs, some of which it is estimated were created in 2,600 BC. Most have now submerged, but one, Spry Island, opposite Kenmore Pier is still visible.

▼ POTTERY

▲ LOCH TAY AND KENMORE

The River Tay flows for 92 miles with Loch Tay accounting for 1/6th of the river's length. The average volume of water flow is a staggering 5614 cubic feet per second which is twice as much as the River Thames giving it the greatest flow of any U.K. river. The Tay is famous for its salmon fishing, and for freshwater pearls, found in mussels in many parts of the river. The largest salmon ever caught in the U.K. with a rod and line, was by Miss Georgina Ballantine, on the Tay in 1922 and was an enormous fish of 64lbs. (30kg.)

Fortingall and Glen Lyon

Lying north of Loch Tay, Fortingall is an attractive village containing several very photogenic cottages which have retained the traditional thatched roofing once widespread in the area. It is often stated that Pontius Pilate was born in Fortingall, and it is certain that there was a Roman presence in the district, as to the south west of the village are earthworks, thought to be the remains of a Roman outpost. One of the most prominent landmarks in the village is the yew tree in the churchyard. This splendid specimen has a girth in excess of 56 feet and is one of the oldest in existence. West of Fortingall, and stretching 25 miles into Breadalbane country, is Glen Lyon. One of the loveliest of all the Scottish glens, and one of the longest, Lyon attracts thousands of visitors throughout the year, particularly in Autumn when the splendour of its colours is reported in the press for "leaf peepers" to catch the best show.

LOCAL FOCUS
or
(Locus)

Based in Aberfeldy, Locus promotes sensitive and sustainable tourism links with the local population. Its intention is not to increase the number of tourists to the area, but to increase the quality of experience for those who visit.

It is a rural development and conservation scheme centred on visitor management by the community. Locus has a number of objectives, aiming to change tourists into visitors, and visitors into informed and returning friends. It seeks to avoid damage to sensitive landscapes and benefit land management initiatives by co-operating with local landowners such as Forestry Enterprise, The National Trust for Scotland and Scottish Natural Heritage; and also by working in conjunction with local authorities to influence provision of car parking, litter bins, maintained footpaths and interpretive centres. As well as promoting a rewarding experience for visitors, Locus provides themed trail packs full of interesting information for self-guided tours within the district. These are aimed at guiding people away from seasonally sensitive sites by providing suitable alternatives. Locus has attracted national and international interest as an example of how a determined rural community can help to maintain its landscape and population, and ultimately its economy.

The Scottish Tourist Board "Oscar" judges were so impressed with this visitor management initiative that they created a special prize for the Locus project.

More information can be obtained from, Locus, The Square, Aberfeldy.

▲ LOCH TAY AND BEN LAWERS

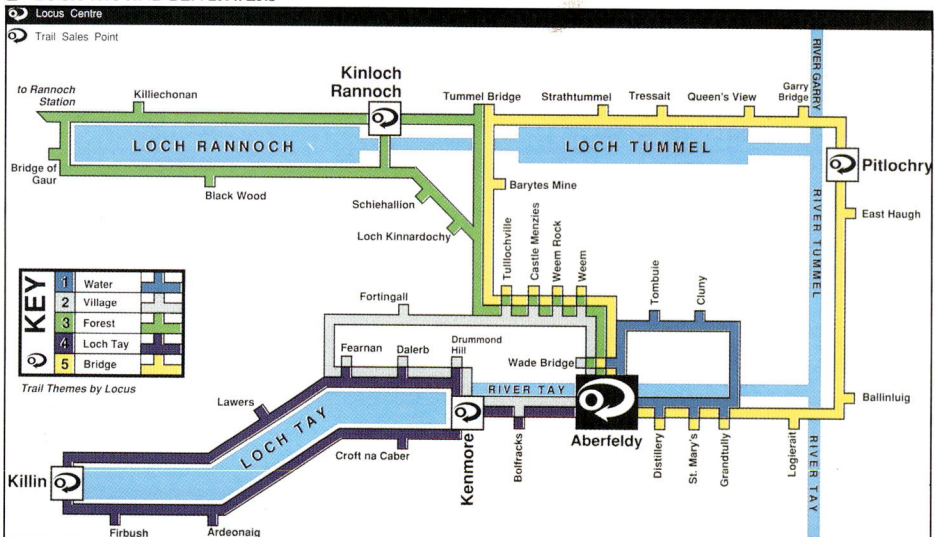

See More With Highland Perthshire's Overground

HILL FARM ▼

BEN LAWERS

Ben Lawers has the distinction of being Perthshire's highest mountain, just 16 feet short of the 4000 feet level. Owned by The National Trust for Scotland since 1950, it has long been a mecca for outdoor enthusiasts. For the naturalist it presents a splendid mountain ecosystem, with regular glimpses of numerous resident creatures, such as red deer, the elusive wildcat, and the raptors - kestrel, buzzards and the magnificent golden eagle. It also boasts one of the finest selections of alpine flowers to be found in Britain. Walkers, skiers and climbers all pursue their sports here, and the first ski tow in Scotland was sited in Coire Odhar, just above the present Visitor Centre, although today there remains no sign of this. The Visitor Centre, 1400 feet up, and its resident Ranger/Naturalist will provide a valuable insight into the botany, geology and wildlife of the area, through the use of static displays and printed material. The Ranger will occasionally lead guided walks to some of the areas of specific natural interest. Due to its popularity amongst visitors from home and abroad, The National Trust has had to undertake a considerable amount of remedial and preventative work to paths on Ben Lawers to minimise damage to the fragile hillside. Whilst the occasional footprint will do little damage, the effect of thousands of feet can wreak havoc. Please play your part in preserving this valuable part of our natural heritage by obeying the signs and keeping to marked footpaths.

GOLF

There are many superb golf courses in Highland Perthshire. Some are on hillsides offering fine views of the surrounding landscape whilst others lie in glens beside rivers or set amidst attractive parklands.

Whatever your standard of golf, from beginner to expert, you will enjoy golfing in the scenic surroundings that the Courses listed here have to offer.

ABERFELDY: Set next to Wades Bridge and the River Tay, and having flat terrain this is also a scenic course.
9-hole course, 5466 yards, (5689 metres), Par of 68, SSS of 67.
Further details from the secretary:
Telephone 0887 820535.

BLAIR ATHOLL: This course lies between the village and the River Garry. Splendid scenic views to Ben Vrackie and the surrounding hills of Glen Garry. The course is set on flat terrain.
9-hole course, 5710 yards.
Par of 69, SSS of 70.
Further details from the secretary:
Telephone 0796 481274

DUNKELD: The course is above the town set in heath land with hilly terrain.
9-hole course, 5264 yards, Par 68, SSS of 66.
Further details from the secretary:
Telephone 0350 727564

KENMORE: Set in parklands, on flat terrain adjacent to Taymouth Castle.
18-hole course, 6066 yards, Par and SSS of 69.
Professional tuition available, Caddy Cars and clubs for hire.
Further details from Director of Golf:
Telephone 0887 830228

▲ TAYMOUTH CASTLE GOLF COURSE

ABERFELDY GOLF COURSE ▼

GOLF COURSE – PITLOCHRY

PITLOCHRY: Set just above the town on the slopes of Ben Vrackie this course offers golfing on hill terrain with superb views of the Tummel Valley and surrounding hills. 18-hole course, 5811 yards, Par of 69, SSS of 68 Professional Tuition available, caddy cars and clubs for hire. During July and August there are a variety of Tournaments. Further details from: Telephone 0796 472792

SPITTAL OF GLENSHEE: This course lies within historic Dalmunzie Estate on mixed terrain.
9-hole hill course, 2035 yards, Par of 30.
Further details from the secretary:
Telephone: 0250 885226

STRATHTAY: Set next to the village this is a 9-hole heath course of mixed terrain, 4082 yards (18 holes) Par of 63.
Further details from the secretary:
Telephone 0887 840367

Highland Perthshire is ideally suited for golfing holidays, with all the facilities for either a short or long stay. Within easy reach are the famous Scottish courses of St. Andrews and Carnoustie, and only forty minutes away by road from Pitlochry is luxurious Gleneagles with its magnificent course. Perthshire takes pride in the choice of facilities it offers the golfer, attracting sportsmen to the district since Victorian times.

▲ PHEASANT

GAME SHOOTING

The habitats of Highland Perthshire are varied: open parklands on the floor of the glens, stands of birch woodland on surrounding hillsides, vast acreages of dense managed forest, and upland moor stretching to the high corries and crags of the mountains. These habitats support a diverse range of animal and bird life, and the sport of hunting has naturally developed in an equally broad manner. Carefully regulated, and managed as a renewable resource, sport shooting is available in many locations throughout the district, and contributes significantly to the local economy. Many hotels and estate agents specialise in catering for shooting parties. For wild birds the main seasons are: Grouse, August to December; Pheasant, October to February; Black Game, August to December; with snipe, woodcock, partridge and duck, amongst others, in season at various times.

Stalking the various deer that inhabit the area takes place throughout the year. It is permitted to take Fallow Does from August to February; Roe Bucks from May to October and the mighty Red Deer stag from July to October. Advice for prospective visitors wishing to go stalking can be obtained from local estates, estate agents, hotels and gunshops, who can also advise on the exact dates when specific game is in season, and any restrictions that may apply.

◄ STAG IN WINTER

▲ FISHING AT DAWN

▲LOCH TAY

RIVER TAY ▼

LOCH and RIVER FISHING

Highland Perthshire offers the visiting angler many opportunities. Dominated by the River Tay, the area is best known for salmon, sea trout and brown trout, although coarse angling is permitted in places. Scotland has its own unique regulations covering the sport and it is wise to be fully acquainted with them. Information, along with the required permits can be obtained from various places, but usually tackle shops, hotels, Post Offices and estate agents can advise.

It should be noted that there is no Sunday fishing for salmon allowed, and should you catch one it must be returned. The salmon and sea trout season extends from 15th January until 15th October inclusive. Wild brown trout can reach 1lb. or more and their season extends from 15th March to 6th October inclusive. Coarse fishing for pike and perch is available, and on one or two river stretches, for grayling, however permits for the latter are not so readily available due to the conflict with game fishing interests. There is no statutory close season for coarse fishing. This is only a brief introduction to the splendid fishing the area has to offer. Whatever style of angling you choose to pursue you are guaranteed some of the finest surroundings in Scotland in which to enjoy your sport. Above all, respect your quarry, respect other people's right to enjoyment, and respect the countryside.

GUIDE TO ADVERTISERS

Tourist Information Centres are able to help with accommodation bookings, holidays, travel information, the ones which relate to the areas covered by this book are listed below:

ABERFELDY, The Square, Aberfeldy PH15 2DD
Telephone 0887 820276

DUNKELD, The Cross, Dunkeld, PH8 0AN
Telephone 0350 727688

PITLOCHRY, 22 Atholl Road, Pitlochry PH16 5BX
Telephone 0796 472215

The contents of this publication are believed to be correct at time of printing, however the publishers cannot be held responsible for errors or omissions and do not necessarily agree with all the views expressed within. Owing to geographical constraints not all of Highland Perthshire is included.